A woman NEEDS A MAN LIKE A CAT NEEDS A BICYCLE

Daisy Hay

summersdale

A WOMAN NEEDS A MAN LIKE A CAT NEEDS A BICYCLE

Copyright © Summersdale Publishers Ltd, 2009

Illustrations by Sarah Horne

Summersdale Publishers Ltd
46 West Street
Chichester
West Sussex
PO19 1RP
UK

www.summersdale.com

Printed and bound by Tien Wah Press, Singapore

ISBN: 978-1-84024-754-1

Substantial discounts on bulk quantities of Summersdale books are available to corporations, professional associations and other organisations. For details telephone Summersdale Publishers on (+44-1243-771107), fax (+44-1243-786300) or email (nicky@summersdale.com).

Contents

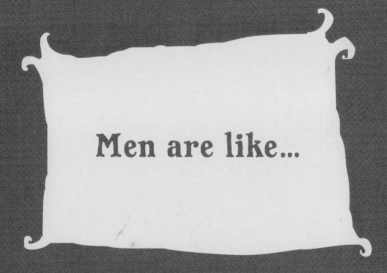

Men are like...

... popcorn

– they satisfy you,
but only for a little while.

... **blenders**

– you've got one in your kitchen,
but you're not quite sure why.

... photocopiers

- necessary for reproduction,
but not much use for anything else.

... horoscopes

- they're always telling you what to do.
They usually get it wrong.

... lava lamps

- nice to look at,
     but a bit dim.

... **carpets**

        – lay them right the first time,
and you can walk all over them for years.

... a tube of suncream

- one squeeze and they're all over you.

... mascara

- at the first sign of tears, they run.

... puppies

- a law unto themselves,
and prone to leaving stains
on your brand new carpets.

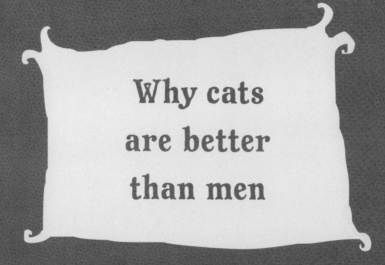

Why cats
are better
than men

In the beginning you might
find them very alike

- they both share a fear of the vacuum cleaner...

... and they both like to fall asleep after a good feed.

But over time you'll start to notice some differences.

After a year, your cat will still be excited to see you when you come home.

Your cat won't reveal that it's
already married to someone else...

... and it's unlikely to
have an obsessive ex-lover.

You can rely on
your cat's loyalty.

It won't run off with
the baby-sitter or cleaner...

... though it may bring the
odd bird home every now and then.

When your cat comes in late,

it won't wake you up by crashing into the furniture...

... because it never fools around with anything stronger than catnip.

A cat might moult from time to time,

but its hairline will never recede...

... and it won't develop a beer belly.

Your cat will never criticise
you for not shaving your legs...

... and will love rubbing up against
them regardless of any cellulite.

It's true that your cat might sometimes have bad breath...

... but at least it won't try to lunge in for an unwelcome snog...

... and that's because, ultimately, a cat knows that you're the key to their happiness, and not the other way around.

Yes, men may come and go, but a cat is for life.

What a man says
and what he
really means

Hello.

= Let's cut the talk and jump straight into bed.

I work in television.

= I sell televisions.

How's your family?

= Is your sister single at the moment?

I'm divorced.

= I just took off my
wedding ring for the evening.

Of course your bum doesn't look big in that dress.

= Please don't try any more outfits on - I'm starving already!

I'm sorry for flirting
with your best friend.

 = I can't believe you caught me!

I like a woman with
a sense of humour.

= If you don't laugh at all my jokes
I will feel like a failure in life and cry.

I eat healthily.

= I eat the gherkins in my BigMacs.

I'm ready for a
meaningful relationship.

= I want lots of sex.

I have my own exclusive studio apartment with 24-hour maid service.

= I live at home and my mum does all my laundry.

Yes, I'd love to go away for a romantic weekend in Germany with you.

= Mmm... Beer.

I can really see myself
settling down with you.

= You seem like a good cook.
Would you like to be my live-in chef?

I can't find my keys!

= I haven't even bothered looking
for my keys – I expect you to
keep track of these things.

I'd explain how it works of course,
but I don't want to bore you.

= I have absolutely no idea how it works.

I don't mind helping
out with the housework.

= I once filled a dishwasher.

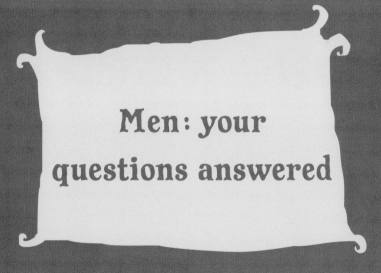

Men: your
questions answered

55

Why are so many sperm released when it only takes one to fertilise an egg?

They won't stop to ask directions.

What makes men chase women they have no intention of settling down with?

The same urge that makes dogs chase cars they have no intention of driving.

Why do all men want to own BMWs?

It's the only car make they
know how to spell.

What's better in bed – ice cream or men?

Ice cream: because you don't have to wait as long for seconds.

What do birthdays, anniversaries, toilets and the point have in common?

Men keep missing them.

What's the best way to persuade a man to do something?

Tell him you think he's too old to be doing it.

How do you get a man to do sit-ups?

Put the remote control between his feet.

How many men does it take to wallpaper a room?

Just one – but you'd have to slice him very thinly.

66

If a man is always well dressed, what does that say about him?

His wife or mother has good taste.

Men: the do's and don'ts

Do move your private emails to a
folder labelled 'Instruction Manuals'.

That way you can be
sure he won't read them.

Do leave the Dial-a-Pizza menu in an obvious place if you leave him at home alone for the weekend

(unless you think his waistline would benefit if he went a couple of days without food).

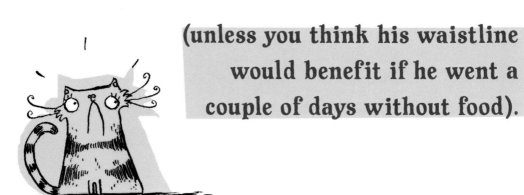

Do ask him to open jars for you

- even though you can do it yourself,
he needs a sense of purpose in life.

Don't hit a man with glasses.

Hit him with a cricket bat.

Do turn the TV off if you need to communicate with him about something important

- unless you just need him to say yes.

Don't tell a man to go
and change the baby

- he'll start thumbing through the
Yellow Pages looking for 'Infant Exchange'.

Don't ever make a fool out of a man

- most are more than capable of
doing that themselves.

Don't bother with the housework

- no man ever fell for a woman because her house was spotless.

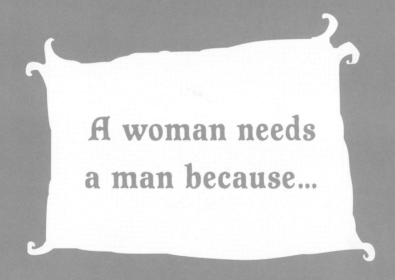

A woman needs
a man because...

... it's nice to have someone to
blame for those dubious smells,

especially if you don't own a dog.

... **shopping bags don't carry themselves.**

... changing a tyre would play havoc
with your French manicure.

... though cumbersome, they make excellent draught excluders.

... they keep the sides of the sofa well stocked with loose change.

... they make you look good on the dance floor.

... it only takes one to screw in a light bulb:

men will screw anything.

... they have pockets.

And remember...

A man who has everything money can buy
still needs one thing - a woman to
show him how to work it all.

Have you enjoyed this book?
If so, why not write a review on your favourite website?

Thanks very much for buying this Summersdale book.

www.summersdale.com